You have an appointment with **Doctor Dad**™!

When my wife and I were expecting our first child, my wife got a lot of information on how to best care for herself and our baby. We went through childbirth classes to prepare for our new arrival, but then our son came home! I knew our son wouldn't come with an instruction manual, but there were times when my wife and I wished he had. A manual that outlined the essential health and safety information needed to care for our son would have been very helpful.

Our son is now in his twenties and there still isn't a manual, but I'm excited to say that there is a workshop, and you're in it! Welcome to **Doctor Dad**™. During **Doctor Dad**™, you'll learn "the basics" to promote health, identify and treat illness and prevent injury. While the workshop targets infant and toddler health, you'll learn skills that you can build on as your child grows.

Your child needs you to be involved in every aspect of his or her life, and that includes their health and healthcare. When you are involved, your child is much less likely to suffer from an injury and more likely to go to their check-ups to keep them healthy.

I'm excited that you've chosen **Doctor Dad**™ to help build your parenting skills. Good luck and good health.

Best regards,

Roland Warren
President
National Fatherhood Initiative

To Learn More About NFI and the *Doctor Dad*™ Program:

TRAINING, TECHNICAL ASSISTANCE, AND QUESTIONS ABOUT THE DOCTOR DAD™ PROGRAM

Phone: (301) 948-0599
Fax: (301) 948-4325
Email: healthcare@fatherhood.org
Website: www.fatherhood.org

National Fatherhood Initiative℠

LEARN MORE ABOUT NATIONAL FATHERHOOD INITIATIVE

101 Lake Forest Boulevard, Suite 360
Gaithersburg, MD 20877

Phone: (301) 948-0599
Fax: (301) 948-4325
Email: info@fatherhood.org
Website: www.fatherhood.org

First Edition
Christopher Brown, Gordon Duvall, and Yvette Warren.

© 2004 National Fatherhood Initiative   Printed in the United States of America.

ATTENTION: Trademark and Copyright Protection
The manuals, inventories and other instructional materials published by the National Fatherhood Initiative are federally protected against unauthorized reproduction whether print or electronic.

Dads Club™

You're a dad for life, so join the Dads Club™ for life!

SHOW YOUR COMMITMENT. JOIN THE CLUB.

Show your commitment to involved, responsible, and committed fatherhood by becoming a lifetime member of Dads Club™. Give a one-time gift of $30, and you'll receive an exclusive T-shirt, CD-ROM, and more exciting resources!

Call (301) 948-0599 or visit www.fatherhood.org.

WE'RE LOOKING FOR A FEW GOOD MEN... ★★★ TO DO ★★★ DOUBLE DUTY!

DOUBLE DUTY DAD

The Double Duty Dad™ program aims to give experienced fathers a chance to mentor fatherless children and less experienced dads.

★ ★ ★ ★ ★ ★ ★ ★ ★ ★ ★ ★ ★ ★ ★ ★

With just 24 hours a year, you can make a huge difference in the life of a child!

★ ★ ★ ★ ★ ★ ★ ★ ★ ★ ★ ★ ★ ★ ★ ★

To learn more about how you can help, visit
www.doubledutydad.org

FREE! Dad E-mail

Hints, tips, and how to's for dads!

Delivered Wednesdays straight to your inbox.

Get connected today at www.fatherhood.org.

FATHER SOURCE

The Fatherhood Resource Center
www.fathersource.org | 301-948-0599

Need some strategies to help make fathering a little easier?

Check out our innovative resources at www.fathersource.org

Doctor DAD

FATHER'S HANDBOOK

First Edition (Revised) ©2005 National Fatherhood Initiative

www.fatherhood.org

mann
Doctor DAD

FATHER'S HANDBOOK

TABLE OF CONTENTS

INTRODUCTION 1

THE WELL CHILD 5
    Temperament 6
    Crying 8
    Nutrition 10
    Immunizations 14
    Learning Review 15

THE SICK CHILD 17
    Taking A Temperature 18
    Fever 20
    The Common Cold 22
    Preventing Dehydration 24
    Learning Review 26

THE INJURED CHILD 29
    Burns 30
    Sunburns 31
    Drowning 32
    Cuts, Scrapes and Bleeding 33
    Head Injuries 34
    Poisoning 36
    Choking 39
    Learning Review 41

THE SAFE CHILD 43
    Car Safety 44
    Home Safety 46
    Guns 56

   Parental Anger 57
   Learning Review 58

APPENDIX **61**
   Answers to Learning Reviews 63
   How to Sooth a Crying Baby 64
   Emergency Phone Numbers 66
   First Aid Kids 67
   Home Safety Checklists 68
   Go Baby, Go: Stuff for your Diaper Bag 70
   Glossary of Medical Terms 71

The Purpose of Doctor Dad™

The purpose of Doctor Dad™ is two-fold:
1. To increase fathers' parenting skills in the area of infant and toddler health.
2. To help fathers realize that they play a unique role in caring for their children.

Increasing Parenting Skills for Infant and Toddler Health:
Caring for your child's health and safety might not come as easily as we think. Dads don't get a manual when they bring their babies home from the hospital. Doctor Dad™ will cover basic health and safety information that you should know.

Your doctor will spend a lot of time in the first few months of your child's life teaching you about the basics of health and safety. You can partner with your doctor to make sure that your child has a healthy start by learning as many skills as possible during Doctor Dad™.

Did you know that you play a unique role in caring for your children?
Dad's parenting style is different from moms' parenting style. Scientists know that children grow better and can be healthier if you use your unique style.

Did you know that when you are involved in your child's life that your child is more likely to get healthcare and less likely to be injured at home?

Different Parenting Style:
Name a few ways that your parenting style is different from mom's style:

_____

_____

_____

_____

Dads' and Moms' parenting styles are different. One is not better than the other.

REMEMBER!
Your children need your unique parenting style. They will be healthier when you are involved.

THE PURPOSE OF DOCTOR DAD™

Did you know that being involved right from the start affects your child's health for a lifetime?

Health and Healthcare of Children	When Dads Are Involved	When Dads Are Not Involved
Poverty	Children are less likely to be poor.	Children are 5 times more likely to be poor.
Healthcare Visits	Children are more likely to see their doctor for regular check-ups or when they are sick.	Children are less likely to see their doctor for regular check-ups or when they are sick.
Safety	Children have less chance of being in an accident, getting injured or being poisoned.	Children have a 20-30% higher chance of having accidents, injuries or poisonings.
Child Abuse	A father's involvement in the physical care of his child before age 3 reduces the chance that he will sexually abuse his child.	Father absence is one of the most common predictors of child abuse.
Neglect		Risk of neglect is doubled.

During Doctor Dad™, You Will Learn How to:

- Know your child's well temperament
- Take care of your sick child
- Know when to call the doctor
- Handle a medical emergency
- Keep your child safe

These are just a few of the skills that you will learn in Doctor Dad™. You will learn the basics about health and safety. **You will not learn how to be a doctor.** It will be helpful to remember several things as you go through Doctor Dad™:

- **There are no silly questions.**
Be sure to check with your doctor if you have any questions about your child's health.

- **Every child is different.**
You will learn basic information in Doctor Dad™. If your child has special needs, always check with your doctor.

- **Call for help if you have a medical emergency.** You will learn what to do while you are waiting for help to arrive if your child has a serious cut or burn.

First Edition (Revised) ©2005 National Fatherhood Initiative www.fatherhood.org

Medical Disclaimer

The information contained in this book has been prepared by licensed medical professionals; the material therefore conforms to accepted medical practices in most circumstances. However, such information and statements contained here are necessarily general in nature. As such, the information and statements may not be comprehensive nor are they intended to dictate the appropriate course of treatment in all situations. Care or action differing from that derived here may be required either because of differing community standards or because of observations and conclusions, which can only be made on a case-by-case basis.

Always consult your doctor or medical care provider before acting with respect to any individual case.

The National Fatherhood Initiative, its officers, board members, and employees deny any and all liability for any injuries, losses, claims, damages, and expenses arising from or related to the information in this material. Acceptance and use of the information constitutes agreement to this disclaimer of liability.

THE WELL CHILD

The information contained in this section covers **"the basics"** on caring for a well child. You will learn information that helps you understand your child's temperament and why your child might be crying. You will also learn about nutrition and immunizations (shots). **Always** consult your doctor if your child is younger than 3 months old or you have questions about your child's wellness. Remember that all children are different. You might need special ways to care for your child if your child has special needs.

THE WELL CHILD

Temperament

What is temperament?
A child's temperament is his or her inborn "likes and dislikes." It causes the child to respond in certain ways to the world. One child, for example, might become upset and cry when hearing a loud noise, while another will merely startle to the same noise. Some people call this a child's "style."

Why is it important to know your child's style?
Because an "easy going" baby will most likely become an "easy going" child and an "easy going" adult. Knowing your child's style will give you a sketch of your child's personality for years to come.

Knowing your child's style will help you:
Know that your child might be getting sick even before you see the first sniffle. Can you think of a child who is "easy going?" This child usually likes everything and eats everything, but then, suddenly, they just sit around and refuse to play or eat. This change in style can signal to dad that an illness is on the way.

Have healthy expectations about your child's behavior. If you know, for example, that your child is "a difficult baby," and finds change stressful, you will expect your child to cry and fuss when he or she is in a new or unpleasant situation. You will understand why your child reacts that way.

Avoid getting frustrated.
If you know your child's style, you will know your child's likes and dislikes. Knowing your child's style can help you avoid getting frustrated because you know what to expect from your child. Perhaps in some cases, you can just say, "That's just my baby's style."

WARNING!
The "difficult baby" can frustrate any parent. It's key for parents of children with this style to accept that style, to find ways to cope with it. Being able to accept and cope with your baby's style will lessen the risk for abuse.

Notes:

_____

_____

_____

_____

What's Your Child's Style?

The Easy Child 😊

- This child can easily handle change. This child doesn't seem to mind a change in people or places.

- This child is "biologically" regular. This child seems to eat, pee and poop on a regular schedule and without much fuss.

- This child's intensity level is mostly moderate. This child doesn't need much to entertain or comfort them.

The Difficult Child ☹

- This child is the reverse of the easy baby. This child is "strong willed."

- This child finds change difficult and are "biologically" irregular. This child seems to eat, drink, sleep, pee and poop whenever he or she wants to or doesn't want to.

The "Slow-to-Warm-Up" Child 😐

- This child is shy and is slow to warm up and adapt to change.

- This child usually cries when faced with change. But the intensity is low and you can calm this child.

Draw the Face that Best Matches Your Child's Style:

My child is probably a _____ baby because …

_____

_____

_____

_____

THE WELL CHILD

Crying

Crying is Communication:
Every child's method of communication will be crying until the child learns to talk. Generally, language (words you understand) does not start to develop until after age 1. Most children do not speak in sentences that you can understand until they are between 2 and 3 years of age.

Babies cry when they need something.

Make a list of things that your child might need when crying:

1._____

2._____

3._____

4._____

5._____

You can never spoil your child by picking him or her up when he or she cries.

Babies learn to trust you when you help them stop crying. Remember, your child cries when needing something. Your child will learn to trust you when you respond to meet his or her needs.

TIP!
If your baby seems to be in pain, take off all your child's clothes and take a close look at the fingers, toes and diaper area for redness or irritation. Sometimes a hair can wrap tightly around a finger or toe and cause pain by cutting off blood flow.

Call your doctor if you don't know why your child is crying. Your doctor might need to check your child's eyes to make sure they're not scratched or that your child isn't sick.

REMEMBER!
Never Shake Your Child! Each year children die or get brain damage because a frustrated parent or caregiver shook them. It's important to know that all parents get frustrated. But it's never okay to take out frustration on your child.

Soothing a Crying Child

How can you comfort a newborn (birth to 3 months)?

- Pediatrician Harvey Karp recommends The 5 S's (see page 64):
  Swaddling
  Side/stomach position for holding
  Shushing (making a "Shss" sound)
  Swinging
  Sucking (offering a pacifier)

- Offering pacifier:
  If your child is full of milk or formula, offering a bottle can make your baby's tummy hurt. Offering a pacifier can satisfy the sucking reflex.

What other things can dads do to help their baby stop crying?

_____

_____

_____

_____

How can you comfort your baby who is 3 months old or older?

As your child gets older, your child will become more coordinated and mobile. Your child will learn to reach and hold things, and will develop his or her own style.

Your job will be more of a challenge as you try to figure out what your child's crying means.

To comfort an older child, try to:

- Change your child's position: Some children enjoy sitting up while others prefer lying down.

- Move your child around: Try a swing, a bouncy seat or, for an older baby with good head control, an exercise seat (a walker without wheels). Go for a walk in the stroller or a ride in the car seat.

- Distract your child: Turn a light on and off, show your child a mobile or a mirror, sing or use music to occupy an older baby if he or she seems bored.

THE WELL CHILD

Nutrition

Milk, breast or formula, is the ideal food for babies. Milk provides all the calories and nutrients that a baby needs to grow during the first 4-6 months of life.

Your baby should not get any cereal or other foods for the first few months of life, unless your doctor tells you to otherwise.

Breast Milk
What are the benefits of breast milk?

When babies are breast fed:

- They are better protected against infections. Breast milk has "antibodies" (proteins that fight infections). These antibodies protect babies from certain sicknesses in the first few months of life.

- They may be less likely to develop asthma or allergies.

- The bond between mother and child is enhanced.

- Breast milk costs less than formula.

- Breast milk is always ready! There is no need for "middle of the night" bottle warming.

Breast feeding saves families money and helps mothers lose some of the weight they gain during pregnancy. There are many advantages to breast feeding. It's important for fathers to encourage mothers to breast feed so that everyone benefits.

Notes:

_____

_____

_____

_____

Formula
Are there different kinds of formula?

There are 2 kinds of formula: (1) modified cow's milk and (2) soy.

If moms are not breast feeding, most babies are started on cow's milk formula in the hospital nursery. Your doctor might suggest a soy formula if he or she is concerned that your baby does not tolerate cow's milk formula.

Formulas come as "ready to feed" liquids or powders.

Make sure the formula you use is iron fortified.

TIP!
Tips on preparing formula or a bottle:

- Check the expiration date.

- Wash off the top of the can.

- Use a clean can opener.

- Mix the formula exactly as directed.

- Store formula in the refrigerator for up to 24 hours.

- Throw away formula your baby does not finish after 1 hour.

Starting Solid Food

How will I know when my baby is ready to start solid foods?

Babies need to be physically ready to take solid foods. Babies need to be able to:

1. Sit up.
2. Lean forward.
3. Open their mouth when a spoon is presented.
4. Keep food in their mouth.

If your baby pushes food out of his or her mouth, your child is not ready for solid foods. Babies have a reflex called the "tongue thrust reflex" that tells them to push solid things out of their mouth. This reflex goes away at about 4 months.

Most doctors will suggest that you start solid food at 4 to 6 months of age.

Why shouldn't I give my baby solid food before 4 months of age?

- Babies have "baby stomachs." They can't handle the kinds of foods we eat. Formula or breast milk is easy to digest. Some scientists think that babies can get allergies if they eat solid foods too early.

- Babies also have small stomachs. Solid food will quickly fill a baby's stomach. Breast milk and formula are "nutritionally complete" – they have all the nutrients your baby needs to grow. Filling a baby's stomach with solid food might keep them from getting the nutrients they need from breast milk or formula.

Starting Other Liquids

When can I offer juice?

You can start to offer small amounts of juice at 6 months of age. Babies need calories and nutrients from breast milk or formula. As a rule, it is best to offer only one or two ounces of juice a day.

When can I switch from formula or breast milk to regular milk?

Start whole milk at 12 months and 2% milk at 2 years of age. Your baby needs the fat that is in whole milk for his or her nervous system to develop.

Notes:

_____

_____

_____

_____

THE WELL CHILD

Tips on Bottle Feeding

1. Never "prop" a bottle. Babies can get ear infections or swallow too much air if a bottle is propped. Hold your baby when feeding him or her. When you do that, the physical closeness you share builds the daddy-baby bond.

2. Offer 2-3 ounces at a time. Babies from birth to 3 months should be fed small amounts more often than an older child. A newborn's stomach can hold about 2-3 ounces, so dads should offer no more than 3 ounces of milk at every feeding. New babies eat about every 2-3 hours.

3. Burp your baby. Most babies swallow air when feeding. Hold your baby leaning back in your arms and tilt the bottle up. Burp your baby after he or she drinks 2-3 ounces.

4. Don't put cereal into a bottle. You should only put cereal in your baby's bottle when your baby's doctor tells you to do so.

Tips on Starting Solid Foods

1. Start with rice cereal. Rice cereal is the easiest to digest. Follow the directions on the box and mix 1 teaspoon of cereal with breast milk or formula.

2. If your baby does well with cereal after a week, you can try one new item a week.

3. Bland fruits (ones without a lot of taste) like unsweetened applesauce, pears and bananas are good first foods. You can also add yellow and orange vegetables after you try a few fruits.

Tips on Foods to Avoid

1. No honey, eggs, fish, peanut butter, citrus fruits (oranges, grapefruit) or whole milk before age 1.

2. Honey can have the germ that causes "botulism." Eggs, whole milk and fish have complex proteins that babies can't easily digest. Peanuts might cause allergies. Citrus fruits have too much acid for babies.

3. Avoid skim milk before age 2. Most children need whole milk from age 1 to 2 years, unless your doctor tells you otherwise.

4. Don't add salt, sugar or spices to foods.

5. "Low-fat" foods. Children don't need the "additives" in these foods. Also, children under 2 years of age need fat to help their nerves grow.

6. Juice. Avoid more than 2-4 ounces of juice per day until age 1. Babies and toddlers need the calories from breast milk, formula and food to grow. Too much juice can cause diarrhea, malnutrition or low weight in your child.

THE WELL CHILD

Immunizations

When will my child get his or her immunizations (shots)?

Children usually get shots at well child check-ups. You should go with your child to these visits if you can. Your doctor will want to get to know you and will give valuable information about your child's growth at these check-ups.

Children get most of their shots during their first year of life. They usually get their shots:

- Shortly after birth.

- At 2, 4, 6, 12 and 15 months.

- They usually get shots called "boosters" between the ages of 4 and 6 years and again between ages 12-14.

Why should your child get shots?

Name 2 reasons your child should get shots:

1. _____

_____

_____

2. _____

_____

_____

REMEMBER!
The most common side effects of most shots are pain and fussiness. This is a small price to pay for a lifetime of protection from 11 major diseases.

The Well Child Learning Review

Circle the correct answer.

1. Every child's style is different.   True / False

2. I can improve my parenting skills if I know what type of style my child might have.   True / False

3. You can spoil your baby if you hold them too much when he or she cries.   True / False

4. Babies cry because they "need something."   True / False

5. Solid food can be started at 3 months of age.   True / False

6. When my child is 12 months of age, I can switch him or her from formula or breast milk to 2% milk.   True / False

7. The most common side effects of shots (immunizations) are pain and fussiness.   True / False

8. Shots protect your child, even though they can be painful.   True / False

Answers can be found on page 63 in the Appendix.

THE SICK CHILD

The information contained in this section covers **"the basics"** of caring for a sick child when he or she has a fever, a cold or vomiting and diarrhea. **Always** consult your doctor if your child is younger than 3 months old or you have questions about your child's sickness. Remember that all children are different. You might need special ways to care for your child if your child has special needs.

THE SICK CHILD

Taking a Temperature

Types of Thermometers

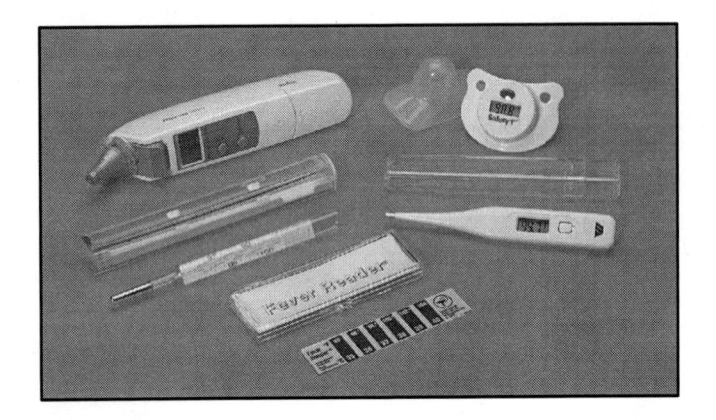

Where can you place a thermometer to take a temperature?

_____

_____

To take a temperature with a strip thermometer:

1. Read the directions on the package.

2. Hold the strip in place until the color stops changing or for the amount of time on the package's instructions.

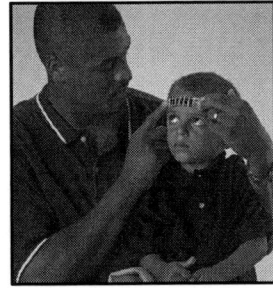

TIP! This is the least accurate way to take a temperature. Never use this way to take a temperature for a baby younger than 3 months or for a child that looks sick.

To take a rectal (bottom) temperature with a digital thermometer:

1. Read the directions on the thermometer package.

2. Turn the thermometer on.

3. Place a probe cover over the tip of the thermometer and place a small amount of petroleum jelly on the tip.

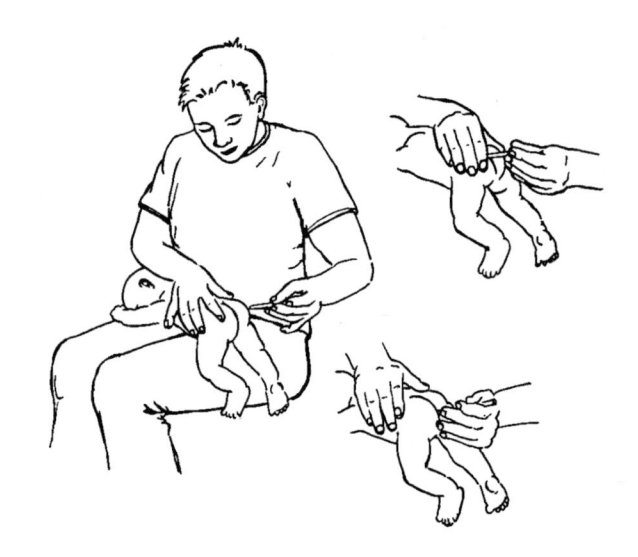

4. Lay your baby on your lap.

5. Steady your baby by placing one hand on his or her lower back and gently spread apart your baby's buttocks.

6. Gently insert the thermometer 1/2 inch into the anus.

7. Hold the thermometer steady until it beeps.

8. Read the thermometer when it beeps.

THE SICK CHILD

To take an oral (mouth) temperature with a digital thermometer:

1. Read the directions on the thermometer package.

2. Turn the thermometer on.

3. Place a probe cover on the thermometer.

4. Have your child open his or her mouth and lift the tongue.

5. Place the thermometer under the tongue and have your child close his or her mouth.

6. Read the thermometer when it beeps.

To take an axillary (armpit) temperature with a digital thermometer:

1. Read the directions on the thermometer package.

2. Turn the thermometer on.

3. Sit your child on your lap or in a comfortable spot.

4. Undress your child or pull his or her clothing up so that the arm and shoulder are bare.

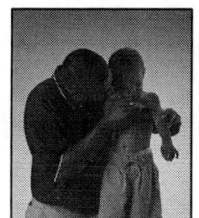

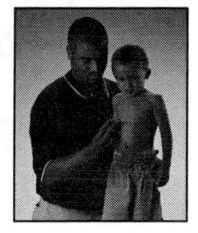

5. Lift up your child's arm. Place the thermometer under the armpit so that it sits in the middle of the armpit.

6. Have your child lower his or her arm and hold it firmly to his or her side.

7. Read the thermometer when it beeps.

To take a tympanic (ear) temperature:

1. Read the directions on the thermometer package.

2. Turn the thermometer on.

3. Gently pull the ear "up and back."

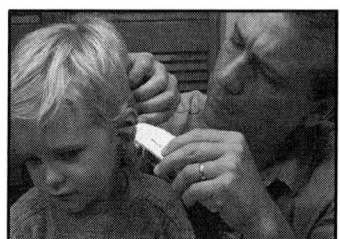

4. Gently insert the thermometer into the ear, but not too far. Placing the thermometer in your child's ear should not cause pain. If it does cause pain, remove it right away.

5. Read the thermometer when it beeps.

THE SICK CHILD

Fever

Normal body temperature is not a single number, but a range: 97 to 100.4 degrees.

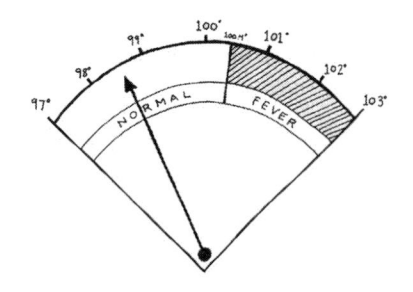

When the body fights an infection, the body's "thermostat" gets "reset" at a higher temperature.

This higher setting is a fever. The body uses this new "thermostat setting" until the infection begins to clear.

What is a fever?

- A fever is an _____ body temperature.

- It is usually a sign that the body is fighting off an _____.

- Fever is not a disease.

- Fever can't harm your child by itself. But you should call your doctor immediately about a fever in babies that are younger than 3 months old and in children with sickle cell or a weakened immune system.

A fever is:

- A rectal (bottom) temperature higher than 100.4 degrees.

- An oral (mouth) temperature higher than 99.7 degrees.

- Axillary (armpit) higher than 99.7 degrees.

Why are temperature readings different depending on where you take them?

Rectal (bottom) temperatures tell us the core body temperature, so they are the most accurate. Your doctor will usually check a rectal temperature on your baby because it is most accurate.

What questions, fears or concerns do you have about fevers?

_____

_____

_____

_____

If all of your questions were not answered today, take your handbook to your child's next doctor visit to have them answered.

! REMEMBER!
Fever is not a disease. It is a sign that your child's body is working.

Calling the Doctor:

Call right away when your child:

- Is younger than 3 months old and has a rectal temperature higher than 100.4 degrees. Sometimes a fever is the only signal that a baby has a serious infection. Always call your doctor if you think your newborn (birth to 3 months) has a fever. Never assume that a fever in this age group is due to teething.

- Has a fever higher than 104, no matter how old he or she is.

- Looks or acts very sick.

Call within 24 hours if:

- Your child has a fever for longer than 24 hours and does not have clear signs of an infection, such as cold symptoms.

- Your child had a fever that went away for 24 hours and returned.

- You have questions or concerns.

Treating a Fever:
What should you know about giving acetaminophen (Tylenol®) to your child for a fever?

- Know your child's most recent weight. The amount of Tylenol® your child should have depends on your child's weight.

- You can give doses every 4-6 hours, if your child seems uncomfortable with a fever.

- If your child had shots in the past 24 hours, Tylenol® will relieve pain.

- If your child has had febrile seizures, talk to your doctor about using Tylenol®

WARNING!
Children's liquid Tylenol® comes in two strengths: "drops" and "liquid." Make sure that you give your child the right strength and amount. Don't use droppers from different strengths of Tylenol®.

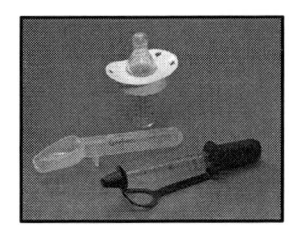

Which tools can I use to give my child medicines? There are many tools that you can use to give your child medicines. The most helpful one is the "syringe" or "dropper" type. Many medicines taste awful, which means that your baby or toddler will spit them out.

- Hold your child snuggly but gently, keeping his or her hands away from the face. An extra pair of hands always helps!

- Place the medicine dropper between the cheek and the tongue and as far back in the mouth as possible without gagging your child.

- Gently squeeze small amounts into the back of the mouth until all the medicine is out of the dropper.

Home Treatment of Fever:
What other things can you do to treat a fever at home?

- Keep your child comfortable. Don't over dress or bundle your child.

- Encourage your child to drink fluids, but don't force your child to drink.

- Don't use alcohol baths or rubdowns. Your child's skin can absorb (take in) alcohol, which can poison your child. Alcohol can also lower a temperature too fast. A sudden, extreme temperature change can be dangerous to your child.

THE SICK CHILD

The Common Cold

Symptoms of the Common Cold

- Watery eyes
- Runny nose and post nasal drip
- Stuffy nose
- Loose cough
- Sore throat

When to call the doctor about cold symptoms:

Situation or Symptom	Why You Should Call
Your child is younger than 3 months old and has other medical conditions (such as prematurity, sickle cell or asthma).	Newborns (babies from birth to 3 months) are looked at a little more carefully by your doctor. Your doctor will make sure that your baby does not need to be examined.
Your child has a cold and has a fever.	Many colds start with 2-3 days of fever, but you also need to remember to use the guidelines that start on page 20 when thinking about calling your doctor.
Your child is having trouble breathing. Look for "retractions": the skin being pulled in between the ribs when a child is working hard to breath. Sometimes a child's nostrils will also "flare" when he or she has trouble breathing.	If your child has a cold and has trouble breathing, your doctor will want to check your child for an infection in the lungs, such as pneumonia.
Your chlid has a cough that lasts more than a week.	Although the most common cause for a cough with a cold is a runny nose, a cough that lasts more than a week might be a sign that there is an infection in the lungs or that your child is wheezing.
Your child has ear pain.	If your child can talk, he or she might tell you that his or her ears hurt. Your doctor might or might not put your child on an antibiotic. Remember, sicknesses caused by viruses (cold germs) are not cured by antibiotics.
Your child is very sleepy or cranky.	Until your child starts to talk, look for changes in your child's style or usual schedule, especially in newborns (birth to 3 months of age).

THE SICK CHILD

Home Treatment
What can you do at home to treat your child with a cold?

_____

_____

_____

_____

What not to do when treating a cold:

- Do not use a "child size" dose of an adult medicine.

- Do not use left over antibiotics.

- Do not share other people's medicines.

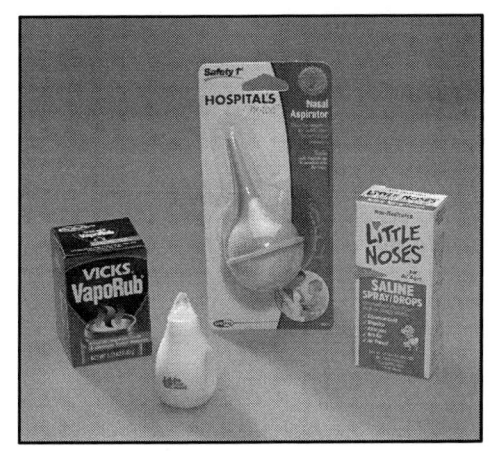

The main signs of a cold are a runny nose or a stuffy nose. You can loosen mucus in the nose with salt water nose drops. You can also use a bulb syringe to pull mucus out of the nose.

Don't forget about Vicks® VapoRub®, which you can put on your child's bib or shirt. The menthol vapors loosen mucus and open a stuffy nose.

TIP!
Use a bulb syringe to clear mucus from the nose:

1. Find a comfortable way to hold your child. If you have a baby, consider swaddling your baby.

2. Squeeze the bulb to let air out of the syringe before placing the tip in your child's nose.

3. Gently place the tip in your child's nose and slowly release the pressure from the bulb. Releasing pressure on the bulb will create suction that will remove mucus. Repeat if needed.

4. Don't forget to wash out the bulb syringe with hot, soapy water after each use.

THE SICK CHILD

Germs

Kinds of Germs:
There are 2 "families" of germs: viruses and bacteria.

Viruses
Viruses are germs that are not alive.

Viruses are like small machines or computer disks that carry information to make you get sick. Once they are in the body, the body starts to fight the infection. As the body fights infection, it makes fever and mucus.

Antibiotics can't kill viruses because viruses aren't alive. You can't kill something that isn't alive. Our bodies use the immune system to get rid of viruses, which can take as long as 10-12 days.

Bacteria
Bacteria are germs that are alive.

You might have heard about common bacteria like streptococcus (strep) and staphylococcus (staph). In general, once bacteria cause an infection, their main symptoms are fever and pain.

Medicines like antibiotics can kill bacteria. It's extremely important that you take an antibiotic exactly as your doctor tells you to. If you don't, the bacteria might not be killed, or it might become resistant to antibiotics.

Differences between viruses and bacteria

Viruses	Bacteria
Not Alive Antibiotics don't kill viruses. Examples: Flu, HIV	Alive Antibiotics will kill bacteria. Examples: Strep, Staph

Notes:

_____

_____

_____

_____

Preventing Dehydration

What is "dehydration?"
Dehydration happens when the body doesn't have enough water to function properly. If water is not replaced after a loss, it can cause decreased activity, weakness and, in extreme cases, death.

What might cause dehydration?
- Diarrhea: Diarrhea is a sudden increase in the number of bowel movements (BMs). It usually causes "runny" or "watery" BMs.

- Vomiting: Vomiting is a forceful emptying of the stomach through the mouth. This is different from "spitting up," which is the release (regurgitation) of small amounts of formula or food from the mouth.

- Improperly mixing formula: Concentrated formulas must have the correct amount of water added to them. Adding too little water might cause dehydration over time.

REMEMBER!
Remember that your child might normally have many small BMs in a day. Breast fed children's BMs are also loose. If you aren't sure whether or not your baby has diarrhea, ask yourself if your baby is having more than their normal number of BMs.

How can I tell if my child is becoming dehydrated?
The best way to tell if your child is becoming dehydrated is to count diapers! The earliest signs of dehydration occur when your child urinates ("wets" or "pees ") less often than normal.

Call your doctor when:
- Your child wets less than 6 diapers in a 24-hour period.

- Hasn't had a wet diaper in the past 6 hours.

- Your child isn't eating.

- Your child is fussy or can't be comforted

WARNING!
Don't wait for your baby to develop late signs of dehydration, such as dry mouth, fewer tears, sunken eyes or soft spot, cool or loose skin before you call your doctor. Your child is very sick by the time these symptoms show up.

The Sick Child Learning Review

Circle the correct answer.

1. If your child is 3 months of age or younger, you should always call your doctor about a fever.   True / False

2. Fever is not a disease.   True / False

3. The most accurate way to take a temperature is in the mouth.   True / False

4. I should call the doctor if my child is 3 months of age or younger and has a cold.   True / False

5. My child will need an antibiotic to kill the germs that cause colds.   True / False

6. I can tell if my child is getting dehydrated by counting the number of wet diapers he or she has in a 24-hour period.   True / False

7. My child is not dehydrated if he or she is wetting 6 or more diapers in a 24-hour period.   True / False

Answers can be found on page 63 in the Appendix.

THE INJURED CHILD

The information in this section covers **"the basics"** of caring for an injured child when he or she is choking or has been burned, cut, poisoned or had a head injury. **Always** talk with your doctor if your child is younger than 3 months old or you have questions about your child's injury. Remember that all children are different. You might need to create special ways to care for your child if your child has special needs.

Burns

What is a burn?
A burn is an injury to the skin caused by heat from fire, hot liquids, chemicals, the sun or electricity. Hot liquids are the most common cause of burns in children. Hot foods, usually found in the kitchen, are very dangerous.

Home Treatment:

1. Run cool water over the burned area for at least 15 minutes. Skin damage can continue even after you remove the cause of the burn. Apply cool water to stop the damage.

2. If the burn blisters, cover it with a non-stick gauze type dressing.

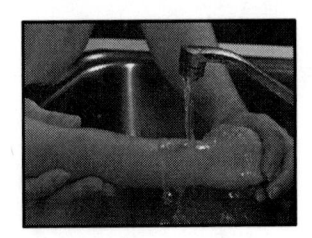

TIP! Use a bowl of cool water instead of running water to treat a burn.

WARNING! Don't use butter, grease or ice to treat a burn.

- Ice can further damage the skin; freezing temperatures can also cause burns.

- Butter, ointments or any grease/petroleum-based product can hold in the heat from the burn and continue to damage the skin.

How long does it take a burn to heal?
A burn should heal in about 7-10 days.

When should I call the doctor for my child's burn?
Call a doctor if a burn looks infected. Look for redness around the burn that gets worse or fluid oozing from the burn that smells bad.

Burns that need medical attention right away:

- Any electrical burn. It is hard to know how bad these burns are until a doctor looks at them.

- Burns on the hands, feet, mouth, face or genitals. Swelling of burns in these areas can cause more injury.

- Burns that ooze pus or have a bad smell. These reactions are signs of a possible infection.

- Redness or swelling that gets worse for 3-5 days after the initial burn. These reactions are also signs of a possible infection.

Sunburns

What should I know about sunburns?

Everyone is at risk for skin damage from the sun, no matter his or her skin color! Even dark-skinned people are at risk of skin damage from the sun. Children are at the most risk for sun damage because they spend a lot more time outdoors than adults: 80 percent of a person's sun exposure comes within the first 20 years of life. Also, children's skin is not as thick as adults, so it raises their risk of sun damage.

WARNING!
Children younger than 6 months of age should not be in the direct sunlight. Their skin is just too thin and too prone to injury to be in the sun.

Skin Protection for Children

Older than 6 Months

- Use sunscreen with an SPF (sun protection factor) of at least 30, and apply it every 2 hours.

- Keep your child out of the sun between 10 a.m. and 3:00 p.m. – this is when the sun is most intense.

- Avoid a false sense of safety from using sunscreen on your child. Limit your child's exposure to the sun.

- Use hats and umbrellas to protect your child from direct sunlight.

Notes:

_____

_____

_____

How can I treat my child's sunburns?

- Apply 1% hydrocortisone cream 3 times per day for 2 days to relieve pain.

- Wet compresses or cool baths with 2 ounces of baking soda added to the water can also give some extra pain relief.

- Get your child to drink plenty of fluids and make sure your child stays out of the sun. If a blister breaks, remove the dead skin with fine scissors. Apply an antibacterial ointment twice a day for three days. If your child has a fever or acts sick, call your doctor.

WARNING!
Don't use Vaseline® or butter on sunburns. These items keep heat and sweat from escaping the skin and they are hard to remove.

THE INJURED CHILD

Drowning

Who is at highest risk for drowning?
Children ages 1-4 and 15-20 are the two groups that are at highest risk. Children in these age groups tend to have "no fear." Toddlers are too young to understand how dangerous water can be. Teens think that accidents can't happen to them.

How fast can drowning happen?
It only takes a few minutes for a child or adult to drown. Sadly, most toddlers were seen less than 5 minutes before they drowned.

Where do most young children drown?
Swimming pools are most dangerous, but it also depends on how old your child is. Children younger than 1 year old drown in 5 gallon buckets, bathtubs and toilets. Babies can drown in less than an inch of water left in the bathtub. Children ages 1- 4 years are at risk of drowning in a swimming pool

> **REMEMBER!**
> You need to know where your child is at all times to prevent drowning!

THE INJURED CHILD

Cuts, Scrapes and Bleeding

You can expect your child to get cuts and scrapes the minute he or she starts to crawl and walk. Most injuries will be minor, but you will need to know basic first aid. The best treatment is to avoid having to treat at all! So, the key is to prevent injury in the first place. Take a fresh look at your home before your child becomes mobile. Remove all items from your home that are breakable or have sharp edges.

Treating Minor Cuts and Scrapes

- Gently clean a minor cut or scrape with soap and water. Don't use iodine, Betadine® or mercurochrome because they destroy skin and cause more harm than good.

- Apply antibiotic ointment and cover the cut or scrape with a non-stick bandage.

When do I need to get medical attention for my child's cut or scrape?
Is the cut or scrape bleeding? If the bleeding is slow and steady, and it slows with direct pressure, it's probably minor. But if the blood is pulsing (coming in spurts) from a cut or scrape, it's probably coming from an artery. **This type of wound needs medical attention right away!**

You might also be able to look at a cut or scrape and tell whether your child needs stitches. If the wound is wide or "gaping," it probably needs stitches.

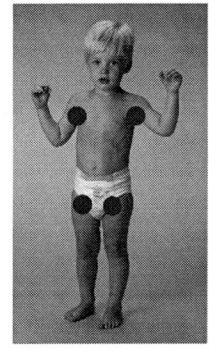

Apply Pressure to the Groin or Armpit
Use direct pressure on a wound to control bleeding, or apply pressure in the groin or the armpit if blood pulsates from a wound. Applying pressure in the groin or armpit helps slow bleeding from an artery.

Notes:

_____

_____

_____

THE INJURED CHILD

Head Injuries

What should I know about head injuries?

- 600,000 children go to emergency rooms each year for head injuries.

- Most head injuries are caused by falls. Most of these falls are preventable.

- The younger the child, the higher the chance of a serious injury.

- Headache, vomiting or blacking out might not be good signs for telling whether a child has a serious head injury.

When should I be concerned about the possibility of a serious injury?
When thinking about whether your child might have a head injury after a fall, you need to think about 3 things:

1. The height from which your child fell.
2. The type of surface fallen onto.
3. The age of your child.

! WARNING!
Serious injury can occur from:

- A fall onto any surface from a height of 3 feet or higher.

- A fall onto a hard surface from less than 3 feet.

- A hard surface is: concrete, wood, solid ground and most surfaces that don't offer a cushion (such as tile floors).

Seek medical attention right away if your child falls and is:

- Younger than 1 year old.

- Not acting him or her self. (A change in your child's style.)

- Unconscious (passed out) after a fall.

When to Call the Doctor

- The fall involves your child hitting his or her head on a hard surface.

- The fall creates a "hematoma" (goose egg). This could mean that your child has a skull fracture, especially if it is behind one of the ears.

- Your child develops bruises around the eyes or ears 24 hours after the fall.

- You have any questions or concerns after your child falls.

What can I do to prevent injuries from falls?

- Don't leave children alone where he or she can fall – not even in a high chair.

- Keep a hand on your baby at all times, especially when changing diapers.

- If your child can pull up to stand, insure safety around cribs.

- If your child crawls or walks, secure stairs with gates at the top and bottom of the stairs.

- Never use walkers that have wheels.

- Never put baby carriers on counter tops, tables or car roofs.

Notes:

_____

_____

_____

_____

Poisoning

Children are most often poisoned by common household items. The most common items that children get poisoned with are vitamins, cosmetics (such as lipstick and perfume) and cleaning products.

Daddy Detective!
Look a little closer! Your child won't tell you if he or she has gotten into something dangerous. So, look for clues that suggest that your child might have gotten into something poisonous.

You should suspect that your child has been poisoned if:

- You find an open or empty container or medicine bottle and you don't know why it's open or empty.

- Your child acts strangely or acts outside of his or her usual style.

- Your child has a stain around his or mouth or on clothes and you don't know how it got there.

- Your child drools or has burns on the lips or inside of the mouth.

- Your child says he or she has a stomach ache, but there isn't a fever.

What should I do if I think my child has been poisoned?

First, don't force your child to vomit. Then take these steps:

1. Take the substance you think poisoned your child away from him or her.

2. Insure that your child is breathing and that his or her airway is clear.

3. Make sure that you have the container that had the substance to let poison control know the substance you think poisoned your child.

4. Call poison control. (Place the number where you get at it easily, such as on your refrigerator.)

5. Do what poison control tells you to do. If they tell you to go to the emergency room, take the container with you.

Notes:

_____

_____

_____

_____

Poison Prevention Tips

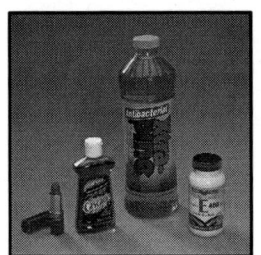

As your child starts to get around and starts getting into things, look for things that can poison your child in your home, the home of friends or relatives, even at the daycare center. Use the tips below to help make your child's world safer. Remember, even when a container is marked "child safe," it doesn't mean that your child can't get into it.

- Keep all medicines, including vitamins, safely locked up, high and out of sight.

- Never call medicine "candy."

- Check with poison control about "safe" houseplants.

- Don't smoke around children and keep tobacco out of reach.

- Never store cleaning products in food containers.

- Keep syrup of ipecac on hand. It helps force your child to vomit. But don't use it unless poison control tells you to do so.

REMEMBER!
You can reach poison control, no matter where you are! Call the 1-800-222-1222 number to connect you to the nearest poison control. Keep this number in your wallet and near the phone.

Lead Poisoning

Lead poisoning is one of the most preventable children's health problems in the United States. High lead levels in the blood can cause a number of symptoms in children, which include: headaches, delayed growth, hearing problems, behavioral problems, difficulty learning and nervous system damage. Most children, however, don't have symptoms. A blood test screens for lead poisoning.

REMEMBER!
Ask your doctor if your child has had his or her lead level checked. This blood work is usually done between the ages of 12 and 24 months—sometimes as early as 9 months.

How do children become exposed to lead?
Lead exposure occurs when children swallow or breathe it in. Lead can be in chips of peeling paint or in paint dust that comes from windows and doors opening and closing.

As your child goes through a stage when he or she puts everything in his or her mouth, your child is at risk for swallowing paint dust or chips that contain lead. Your child can also absorb lead through the skin. So, if your child plays in dirt around older homes, he or she can be exposed.

What are the sources of lead that I should be most worried about?

- Paint dust or chips around windows, doors and soil in homes built before 1978. Most homes built after 1978 won't have lead in the paint because the government banned lead in paint.

- Lead paint on toys from foreign countries.

- Lead from fishing weights.

- Lead glazing on pottery.

- Lead from auto body repair work. (Lead can be on Dad's clothes if he does auto body repair.)

- Lead from water pipes in older homes.

TIP!
If you live in an older home with lead pipes – and if you haven't used your water in the last 2 hours – run your water for at least 2 minutes with cold water before using tap water.

What can I do to reduce the risk of lead poisoning for my family?

- Damp mop floors and wipe down windowsills often to remove paint dust and chips.

- Don't strip old paint. Lead isn't a problem until it's freed into the air as dust or paint chips.

- Don't allow children to play in the dirt around older homes.

- Make sure that your child's diet has enough calcium and iron. These minerals make it harder for the body to absorb lead.

- Call the National Safety Council's Lead Information Center at 1-800-424-LEAD for other ways to reduce the risk.

Notes:

_____

_____

_____

_____

Choking

Why are children more likely to choke than adults?

- Children are more likely to run, talk or play with food in their mouths.

- Toddlers develop their front teeth, the cutting teeth, before they develop the back teeth, which grind food. So they can bite off small pieces of hard food but cannot chew them into a paste to make them safe.

- All children go through an "oral stage" when they put almost anything in their mouths.

What is a choking emergency?
Choking emergencies are when a child can't breathe or turns blue. The child's airway is probably blocked.

What can I do to prevent my child from choking?
Choking is the most preventable cause of death in children under 1 year of age. Children under 1 are at the greatest risk for choking. You can help prevent choking by:

- Being trained in baby and child CPR.

- Knowing the Heimlich maneuver.

- Knowing that the most commonly choked on items are round foods.

Foods to avoid until 4 years of age:

- Peanuts and hard candy.

- Whole grapes and hot dogs. (It's okay to cut these foods into small pieces. But make sure that the pieces are not round.)

- Popcorn.

- Carrots or celery sticks.

Non-food items to avoid until age 8:

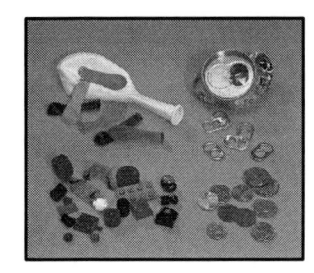

- Coins and small toys.

- Balloons and medical gloves.

- Egg shells and pop-tops from cans.

What can I do to help a child who is choking?

For babies (younger than 1 year):

1. Place your baby face down on your arm.

2. Give 5 back blows between your baby's shoulder blades using the heel of your hand.

3. Turn your baby on his or her back and give 5 upwards stomach thrusts using 2 fingers.

4. If you are alone, take your baby with you to the phone and call 911.

5. Repeat steps 1-3 until your baby coughs or starts to cry.

For children older than 1 year:

1. 5 quick abdominal thrusts (Heimlich).

2. Call 911 and repeat an abdominal thrust until your child coughs or can speak.

THE INJURED CHILD

3. Remove the object from your child's mouth only if you see it.

WARNING!
Only remove the item your child choked on if you see it. Don't try to remove any objects that you can't see. You could push it further down your child's windpipe, which is about as small as the size of a straw.

The Injured Child Learning Review

Circle the correct answer.

1. The most important first step to treat a burn is to run the burn under cool water. — True / False

2. It's okay to use ice, grease or butter to treat a burn. — True / False

3. Babies under 6 months of age should not be in direct sunlight. — True / False

4. Children ages 1 through 4 are at greatest risk of drowning. — True / False

5. Children younger than 1 year old are more likely to suffer from a head injury from a fall onto a hard surface than are older children. — True / False

6. I should call poison control immediately if I think that my child has been poisoned. — True / False

7. I should ask my doctor for a lead test when my baby is 6 months old. — True / False

8. Most children choke on small, round objects. — True / False

Answers can be found on page 63 in the Appendix.

THE SAFE CHILD

The information in this section covers **"the basics"** on creating a safe home and surroundings for your child. **Always** consult your doctor if you have questions about creating a safe home and surroundings. Remember that all children are different. You might need to create special ways to create a safe home if your child has special needs.

THE SAFE CHILD

Car Safety

What can I do to make my child safe in the car?
Make sure that you secure your child in the appropriate safety seat.

	Babies	**Toddlers**	**Young Children**
Weight	Birth to 1 year old, **and** at least 20 pounds	Older than 1 year **and** over 20 pounds	Over 40 pounds, ages 4-8, less than 4 feet and 9 inches tall
Type of Seat	Rear-facing	Forward-facing	Belt-positioning booster seat
Seat Position	Rear-facing	Forward-facing	Forward-facing
Remember!		Harness straps should be at or above shoulders.	Belt-positioning booster seats must be used with both lap and shoulder belts. Make sure the lap belt fits low and tight across lap and upper thigh area. The shoulder belt should fit snugly across the chest and shoulder.

THE SAFE CHILD

Identify Safe and Unsafe Situations in the Car

Write the Correct Weight and Age Ranges for Each Car or Booster Seat

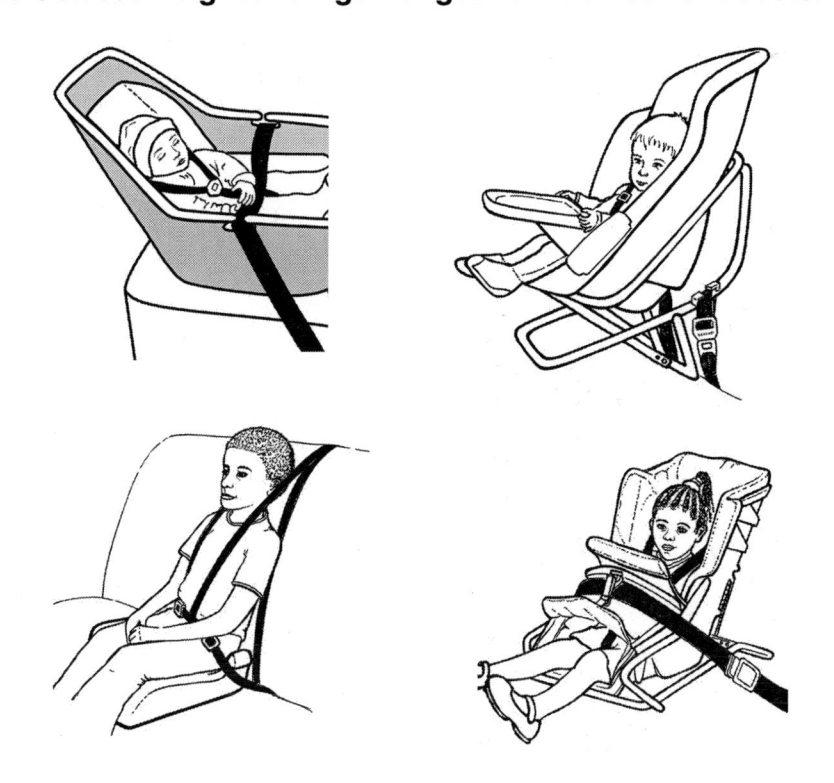

THE SAFE CHILD

Kitchen Safety

Identify Safe and Unsafe Situations in the Kitchen

THE SAFE CHILD

Bathroom Safety

Identify Safe and Unsafe Situations in the Bathroom

THE SAFE CHILD

Bedroom Safety

Identify Safe and Unsafe Situations in the Bedroom

SIDS

What is SIDS?
Sudden Infant Death Syndrome (SIDS) is the leading cause of death in babies between the first month and the end of the first year of life. Sadly, no one knows the cause of SIDS.

How can I prevent SIDS?
Gladly, we do know that fathers can reduce the risk of SIDS by:

- Placing babies on their backs to sleep.

- Having mothers not smoke while pregnant and no smoking by either parent in the home after the baby is born.

- Encouraging mothers to get prenatal care from the moment they know that they are pregnant.

What is the best position for my baby to sleep in?
The best position is on his or her back. In 1993 the American Academy of Pediatrics started their "Back to Sleep" campaign. They said that, to lower the risk of SIDS, all babies should be placed on their backs to sleep. The SIDS rate has been greatly reduced since the start of this campaign.

Suffocation
Suffocation isn't the same as SIDS. Suffocation occurs when the airway or face is blocked or covered. You can prevent suffocation in your children.

How can I lower the risk of my child suffocating?

- Don't let your child sleep on a waterbed.

- Don't place your child on beanbags chairs.

- Don't place pillows in your child's crib.

- Don't place your child on a couch to sleep.

- Don't sleep in the same bed with your child, especially if you or mom has been using alcohol or drugs.

WARNING!
Babies might not start to roll over until age 4-6 months. If they are placed on a soft surface, they will not be able to turn over, which places them at higher risk for suffocation.

What can I do to make a crib safe?
Make a few simple measurements. Crib rails should be at least 26 inches from the top of the mattress. Bars should be no more than 2 3/8 inches apart (the width of a soda can). The mattress should fit snuggly in the crib with no room for your child to get between the mattress and rails. Position the crib away from windows and radiators.

THE SAFE CHILD

Living Room Safety

Identify Safe and Unsafe Situations in the Living Room

THE SAFE CHILD

Yard Safety

Identify Safe and Unsafe Situations in the Yard

THE SAFE CHILD

Gun Safety

Notes:

What do dads need to know about gun safety?
In 1997 there were 32,436 deaths caused by guns in the U.S; 4,223 of the victims were children and teens under age 20.

Children who were involved in accidental gun injuries were more likely to be boys who were playing at home with friends and were not being watched by an adult.

What can I do to make my home "gun safe?"
The best way is to not have a gun in the home. If you decide to keep guns in your home,

- Keep them in a locked area, away from children.

- Keep safety trigger locks on them, even when stored in a locked area.

- Keep ammunition stored in a different place than a gun, also in a locked area.

- Never let your children know where the gun or ammunition is stored.

Parental Anger

It's important to know that we all get angry at times. Anger is a normal emotion that all parents have. The key is to know how to handle anger and frustration when it occurs.

It's also helpful to know your child's style, and to have realistic expectations about your child's behavior.

If you know, for example, that your child is "a difficult baby," and finds change hard, you will expect your child to cry and fuss when he or she is in a new or bad setting. You will also know why your child reacts the way that he or she does.

What can I do to make my child's world calmer?

1. Turn off TV's, radios, video games or other sources of noise.

2. Play calming music.

3. Turn down the lights.

4. Speak in a soft whisper or hum a song for your child.

Make a plan about how you will handle your anger if you think it's getting out of control.

Some things you can do to handle your anger include:

- Call someone you can talk to or someone who can give you a break.

- Put your child in a safe place like the crib or playpen and go into another room for a short time and get yourself together.

- Promise yourself that you will never shake your baby. Shaking your baby can cause brain damage or death.

REMEMBER!
Children have fragile bodies and emotions. So remember:

- Don't yell at them.

- Don't shake them.

- Don't abuse them with harsh words.

- Children watch what you do, so you will teach your child to yell and hit if that is how you handle anger.

Notes:

_____

_____

_____

_____

The Safe Child Learning Review

Circle the correct answer.

1. I can keep my child safe in the car if he or she needs to sit in my lap.　　　　　　　　　　　True / False

2. As soon as my child turns 1 year old, I will be able to put my child in a forward-facing car seat.　　True / False

3. I can help prevent burns in the kitchen by turning pot handles towards the back of the stove when cooking.　True / False

4. One of the best ways to keep the bathroom safe is to keep the door closed.　　　　　　　　　　True / False

5. I can lower the risk of SIDS in my child by encouraging his or her mom not to smoke.　　　　　True / False

6. Placing my baby on his or her back when he or she sleeps is another way to lower the risk of SIDS.　True / False

7. All parents get angry and frustrated sometimes with their children, but I know that I should never shake my child.　True / False

8. Shaking my child when I am angry can cause brain damage or death in my child.　　　　　　　True / False

Answers can be found on page 63 in the Appendix.

APPENDIX

Learning Review Answer Keys

The Well Child Learning Review Answers
1. True.
2. True.
3. False. You cannot spoil your child by picking him or her up or attending to his or her needs when crying. Crying is the only way a baby can communicate that he or she needs something. Responding to cries helps your child learn to trust you.
4. True.
5. False. Solid food should not be started until babies are 4 months of age or older. Starting solid foods earlier than 4 months of age might cause your baby to develop food allergies.
6. False. You should switch your child to whole milk at age 1 year. Toddlers need the additional fat that is in whole milk to help their nervous system develop. 2% milk should be started at age 2 years.
7. True.
8. True.

The Sick Child Learning Review Answers
1. True.
2. True.
3. False. The most accurate way to take a temperature is in the rectum (bottom).
4. True. Children younger than 3 months of age fall into a "special" category and get "special" attention. You should always call your doctor when a child this young gets sick.
5. False. The germs that cause colds are called viruses. Antibiotics kill bacteria not viruses.
6. True.
7. True.

The Injured Child Learning Review Answers
1. True.
2. False. Ice will further damage the skin and butter and grease keep heat in the skin.
3. True.
4. True.
5. True.
6. True.
7. False. Lead testing is done between 9 and 15 months of age. If your child does not get paperwork for blood work at his 1 year check-up, ask your doctor about lead testing.
8. True.

The Safe Child Learning Review Answers
1. False. You can never keep your child safe in the car while he or she sits in your lap. Each year thousands of children die because they are not properly restrained in a car seat.
2. False. Your child must be 1 year **and** weigh 20 lbs. to be safely moved to a forward-facing car seat. If your child turns 1 year of age and has not reached the 20 lb. mark, he or she must stay in a rear-facing infant seat.
3. True.
4. True.
5. True.
6. True.
7. True.
8. True.

The Five S's

Dr. Harvey Karp recommends "The Five S's" to soothe a newborn baby. In "The Happiest Baby on the Block" (www.thehappiestbaby.com), he talks about how to "switch-off" your baby's crying using the following techniques.

The Five S's are great for soothing your baby during his or her fussy times. They trigger the calming reflex—the automatic "off" switch for crying. As you do the Five S's, remember these important points:

- Calming your baby is like dancing, but you have to follow your baby's lead.

- Do the Five S's vigorously only lessening the intensity after the baby begins to settle.

- The Five S's must be done exactly right for them to work.

Here's a summary of the most important aspects of the Five S's that will help you become the "best baby-calmer on the block"...

Swaddling

Don't worry if your baby's first reaction to wrapping is to struggle against it. Swaddling might not instantly calm the fussiness. But what it will do is restrain that uncontrolled flailing. Then your baby can pay attention to the next S's you do, which will switch the calming reflex "on" and guide your baby into sweet serenity!

Step 1:

Step 2:

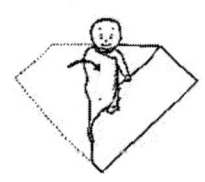

Step 3:

Step 4:

Step 5:

Side/Stomach

The more upset your baby is, the unhappier he or she will be on his or her back. Rolling your infant onto the side or stomach is the way to go. This simple trick can sometimes activate a baby's calming reflex…within seconds.

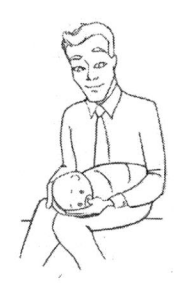

WARNING! Do not put your baby to sleep in a crib on the stomach. Sleeping prone (on their stomach) is considered a risk factor for SIDS.

Shhhh!

Shushing crying babies magically makes them feel at peace, like they were in the womb, but you've got to do it about as loud as your baby's crying and close to the ear …or your baby won't even notice it. Use this super-effective "S" to keep baby calm throughout this fussy period with the aid of a radio tuned to loud static, a tape recording of your hair drier or a white noise machine.

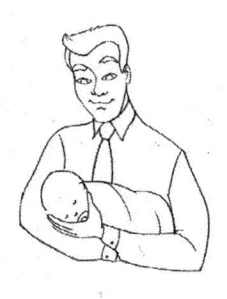

Swinging

Like vigorous shushing, little jiggling movements can turn your baby from screams to sweet serenity in minutes…or less. As you carefully support your baby's head and neck, move baby's upper body with quick but **tiny** movements, sort of like you're shivering. Once calm, you can transfer baby's wrapped body into a swing for steady motion. (Make sure the strap is between your baby's wrapped legs, the swing is fully reclined and it's set on the fastest speed.)

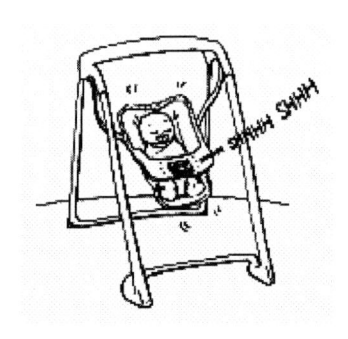

Sucking

This last "S" usually works best after you have already lead your little one into calmness with the other "Ss." Offering a pacifier will be the icing on the cake of soothing. You can teach your baby to keep the pacifier in by using "reverse-psychology" – the moment baby begins to suck on the pacifier, gently tug on it as if you're going to take it out. Baby will suck it in harder and soon will soon learn to keep it in his or her mouth even when cooing.

The content of the 5 Ss are Copyrighted © Dr. Karp 2002 and have been used with his permission.

APPENDIX

Important Phone Numbers

Child's Name:_____
Date of Birth:_____
Most Recent Weight:_____
Allergies:_____

Our Phone Number:_____
Our Address:_____
_____
_____

Family Doctor:_____
Friends and Family:_____
_____
_____
_____
_____

POLICE: 911 or _____
FIRE: 911 or _____
POISON CONTROL: 1-800-222-1222

Child's Name:_____
Date of Birth:_____
Most Recent Weight:_____
Allergies:_____

Our Phone Number:_____
Our Address:_____
_____
_____

Family Doctor:_____
Friends and Family:_____
_____
_____
_____
_____

POLICE: 911 or _____
FIRE: 911 or _____
POISON CONTROL: 1-800-222-1222

Use a pencil to record your child's most recent weight.
Cut around dotted line and keep near your phone.
If you have more than two children, make more copies of this page.

First Aid Kits

Be prepared! A well stocked first aid kit is a handy thing to have around before you need it. Keep the items in a box, safely stored out of reach from children. You can make smaller kits to keep in the car or to take on a trip. You can pack these items in a tackle box or any container. Even a large Ziploc® bag will do!

Most babies and toddlers will only sustain minor injuries. You can usually take care of these "ouchies and boo boos" with common sense, basic medical information and the items suggested in the first aid kit.

You can start a "Baby Basic" Kit. Items in a basic kit are used when your child is sick. Infants who are not crawling or walking won't be getting cuts and scrapes, so you will not need other items right away. You can add to your child's kit as he or she grows.

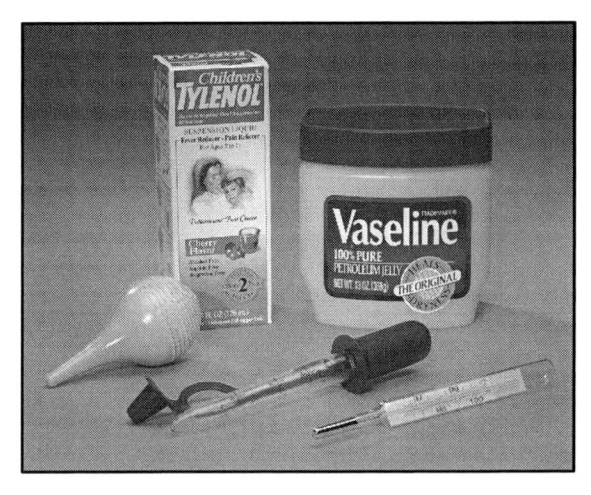

Baby Basic Kit (Birth to 6 months)
Digital thermometer
Vaseline® as lubricant for thermometer
Bulb syringe nasal aspirator
Saline nose drops
Medicine dispenser—dropper type
Liquid acetaminophen (Tylenol®)

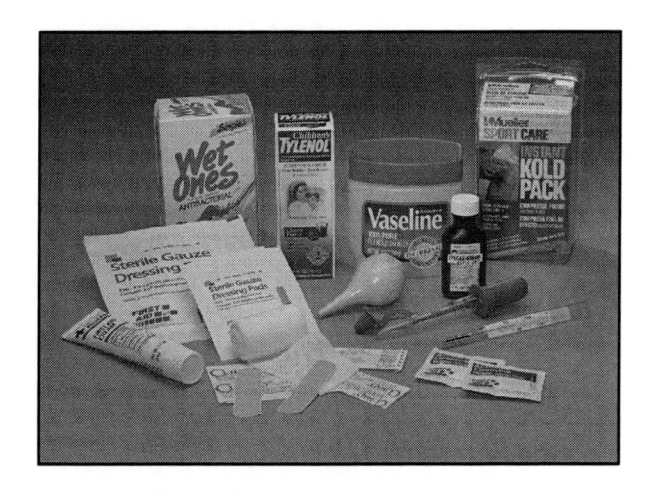

First Aid Kit for Older Children
Band-Aid®s
Antibiotic ointment
Baby wipe packet
Gauze roll; 2x2 gauze pads; 4x4 gauze pads
Q-tips® to apply ointment
Reusable combination hot & cold pack
Syrup of ipecac
A list of important phone numbers

APPENDIX

Room Safety Checklists

Nothing guarantees your child's safety like watching your child, but don't think that watching your child is enough. Think about what your baby is doing now, what he or she will be doing next and where he or she might be doing it. You should get on the floor to get a "child-size" view on his or her world.

Kitchen
- [ ] Clear counter
- [ ] Appliances put away when not in use
- [ ] No loose cords
- [ ] Oven/stove locks
- [ ] Cabinets secured
- [ ] Handles of pots turned to rear of stove
- [ ] Remove tablecloth
- [ ] Trash secured and out of reach
- [ ] Pet food/water put away
- [ ] Knives & sharp items put away
- [ ] Cleaning supplies out of reach or locked
- [ ] Electric socket covers in place

Never leave your child alone in your kitchen.

Bathroom
- [ ] Electric socket covers in place
- [ ] Electric appliances put away
- [ ] Cleaning supplies put away
- [ ] Toilet lid lock in place
- [ ] Shaving accessories put away
- [ ] Medications/cosmetics out of reach
- [ ] Non-slip tub mat
- [ ] Faucet cover/padding
- [ ] Hot water heater set below 120 degrees

Never leave your child alone, and keep the bathroom door closed, if possible.

Bedroom
- [ ] Snug-fitting crib mattress
- [ ] No pillows or stuffed animals in crib
- [ ] Working smoke detector
- [ ] Electric socket covers in place
- [ ] Window blind cords tied up and out of reach
- [ ] Radiator/heater covered
- [ ] Safe toy box, no heavy lid
- [ ] Crib away from window
- [ ] Window secured, gated if above 1st floor
- [ ] All baby care supplies put away

Never leave your child alone in the bedroom.

Living room
- [ ] Working smoke detector
- [ ] Electric socket covers in place
- [ ] Bookcases secured to wall
- [ ] Knick-knacks put up out of reach
- [ ] Houseplants placed out of reach
- [ ] Electric cords taped down
- [ ] Curtain cords tied up and out of reach
- [ ] Door lock out of reach
- [ ] Table corners padded
- [ ] Gates at top and bottom of stairs
- [ ] Pictures/mirrors out of reach
- [ ] Electronic equipment out of reach

Never put an infant to sleep on the couch or leave your child alone in the living room.

Garage
- ☐ Put tools up out of reach
- ☐ Lock/secure toolboxes
- ☐ Put chemicals away
- ☐ Unplug electric tools
- ☐ Secure all electric cords
- ☐ Working smoke detector
- ☐ Put away lawn mower and other lawn tools

Never leave your child alone in the garage.

Outside of House
- ☐ Identify and eliminate poisonous plants
- ☐ Avoid strange pets & animals
- ☐ Clean up trash
- ☐ Put away pet food & water
- ☐ Lock gate
- ☐ Secure pool with locking gate
- ☐ Safety seats for swings
- ☐ Put away all tools

Never leave your child alone outide your home.

Car
- ☐ Working seat belts
- ☐ Proper sized car seat
- ☐ Emergency kit
- ☐ First aid kit
- ☐ Cell phone
- ☐ Safe treaded tires
- ☐ Put dangerous items out of reach

Never leave your child alone in the car, especially when it's hot outside.

Go Baby Go

You can take your children just about anywhere. The keys to making a trip run smoothly are planning and a well packed diaper or activity bag.

Planning Ahead
Planning ahead doesn't just mean packing. It means knowing your child's style and schedule. Tiredness, hunger, health and time of day affect both parents and children.

Planning Tips:
- Try not to schedule an activity during your baby's dinner time—unless you were planning on having a picnic.
- Always pack a snack.
- If your baby is an active child, plan to have a few toys or books to help keep him or her busy and happy.
- Don't forget the stroller. Changing a child's position can often keep him or her happy.

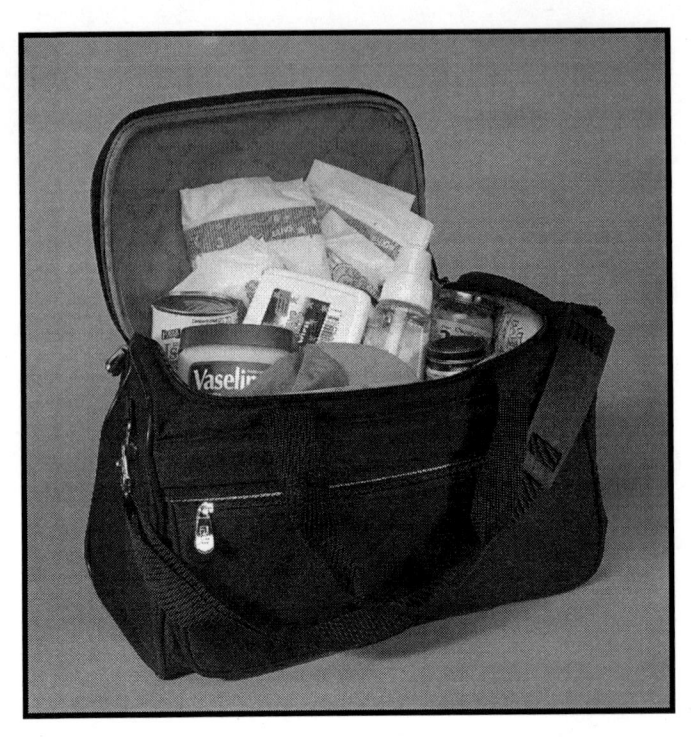

In the Bag
Choose a bag that meets your needs. Sometimes a backpack is all that's needed. Ziploc® bags are a great way to pack items.

Things to pack:
- Diapers, wipes and diaper ointment
- Changing pad or small towel
- Change of clothing for your child
- Plastic bags for wet clothes
- Baby foods, bottles (ready to feed, single serving pouches are now available) or a sipper cup for an older child
- Snacks: finger food like cheerios, gold fish, saltine crackers
- Pacifier
- Special blanket or toys
- Books
- Important medical and emergency information

Glossary of Medical Terms

This glossary defines helpful terms related to the health and wellness of your child. You might find some of these terms used in your handbook. There are other terms included that are not in the handbook, but are useful terms to know.

Adverse Reaction: A response to a medicine or treatment that is acting against or in the wrong way, <u>unfavorable</u>, not what was meant to happen.

Ambulatory Care: Medical care received outside of the hospital. For example, well child check-ups, routine physicals, etc.

Antibiotic: A medicine used to fight or kill a disease caused by bacteria. Antibiotics will not kill viruses.

Antibodies: Proteins that are the basis for the human immune system. Antibodies are proteins made by the body after exposure to an illness or vaccine. Antibodies are used by the body to fight infection.

Asthma: A disorder marked by difficulty in breathing, wheezing and coughing. Asthma is often caused by allergies.

Asymptomatic: No symptoms; being without a sign that reveals a disease or abnormality.

Autism: A mental disorder starting in infancy that is characterized esp. by an inability to interact socially, repetitive behaviors and language disorders.

Botulism: A disease caused by a bacteria often found in tainted foods.

Calories: The units for measuring heat; used on food labels to tell how much energy is found in a food.

Cognitive Development: The growth of one's mental skills, such as thinking, remembering, learning and language.

Congenital Rubella: German Measles existing at or dating from birth.

Diphtheria: A very bad infection that usually attacks the throat and nose. It is easily passed from one person to another and can kill someone. In more serious cases, it can attack the nerves and heart. Because of widespread immunization, diphtheria is very rare in the United States. Some people, however, don't get the shot to prevent diptheria, so cases still occur.

Electrolyte Imbalances: The loss of body fluids due to lots of vomiting, diarrhea, sweating or high fever can lead to imbalances of electrolytes. Electrolytes can carry an electrical charge. They are found in the blood, tissue fluid and cells of the body. Common electrolytes in the body include sodium, potassium, calcium and magnesium. Imbalances in any of these electrolytes can result in serious health problems.

Failure to Thrive: Failure to thrive describes children whose current weight or rate of weight gain is far below that of other children of similar age and sex.

Father Hunger: Sleep disturbances, such as trouble falling asleep, nightmares and night terrors often begin one to three months after father leaves the home. Often afflicts boys 1 to 2 years of age whose fathers leave suddenly.

Fever: A rise in body temperature above the normal, which is defined as a range, not a single number.

APPENDIX

Forage: To search for food or supplies.

Hydrocortisone Cream: Steroid cream that decreases inflammation.

Hypoxia: To not have enough oxygen in blood/system.

Immune system: The system that protects the body from foreign substances, cells and tissues by producing the immune response, which fights off infections. This system includes the thymus, spleen, lymph nodes and lymphocytes.

Immunizations: Substances given to make a person immune to a particular illness. Can be given by mouth or injected, depending on type.

Infected: Being affected by a disease or condition caused by a germ or parasite.

Infectious Diseases: A condition caused by a germ or parasite causing an abnormal bodily condition that impairs functioning and can usually be recognized by signs and symptoms that present as a sickness.

Intracranial: Inside the skull; enclosing the brain.

Intravenous fluids: Fluids being given by way of the veins. Fluids may be administered for fluid replacement due to dehydration or for administration of medication/nutrients.

Malnutrition: Faulty and especially inadequate nutrition.

Mercurochrome: A solution of iodine used as a local antiseptic.

Misconception: The process of not conceiving or not being conceived. The inability to form or understand ideas or concepts.

Morbidity: The incidence of disease, the rate of sickness (as in a specified community or group).

Mortality: The number of deaths in a given time or place. The proportion of deaths to population, the **death rate**.

Nurturance: The promotion of growth and development of all of one's traits, qualities and characteristics.

Nutrition: The act or process of nourishing; especially the processes by which a person takes in and uses food.

Prone Positioning: Lying face down, on stomach.

Psychologist: A person trained to study the science of mind and behavior.

Pyloric Stenosis: A condition that affects the gastrointestinal tract during infancy; a narrowing of the outlet of the stomach. This condition can cause your baby to vomit forcefully; may cause other problems such as dehydration and salt and fluid imbalances.

Reactive Airways: (See **Asthma**)

Rhinorrhea: Nasal discharge, usually mucus; material that comes out of the nose.

Seizure: A sudden attack that affects the central nervous system causing an abnormal and violent involuntary contraction or series of contractions of muscle.

Septic Work-up: A procedure used to identify the cause of sepsis, which is an infection that affects the entire body. The work-up could include but is not limited to: blood & urine cultures, spinal tap and throat cultures.

Solid Foods: Nutrition for the body that is not liquid.

SPF: (Skin or sun protective factor) a rating scale for the strength of sunscreen.

Stature: The natural height of a person.

Suffocation: The act or result of being stifled, smothered or choked.

Tetanus: An infectious disease caused by bacterial poisons and marked by muscle stiffness and spasms especially of the jaws.

Trachea: The main tube by which air enters the lungs; windpipe.

Tympanic thermometer: Takes the temperature measurement from the eardrum.

Vaccines: A single or group of materials (as a preparation of killed or weakened virus or bacteria) used in vaccinating to induce immunity to a disease.

Virus: Any of a large group of submicroscopic infectious agents that can grow and multiply only in living cells, and that cause diseases.